Published by Naked Cat Publishing
https://nakedcatpublishing.myshopify.com/

CHERRY SPITTER

a diary and recounting of a recovering alcoholic, ex-stripper in the midsouth

A chapbook by: Lin Elizabeth

TABLE OF CONTENTS

The Sacrality of The Pig

At the meek waitressing job while you were 'tapering' at your father's house before caving and moving back into your mother's—

You flirted with the very married cook, innocently, because he was nice and passionate about cooking.

You wore passion around your throat. He wanted to do nothing but work for himself.

You knew that cross. you've bore that.

Jesus, both were akin to the hike.

You never meddled. Only genuine questions of interest:
How Do I Make Tomato Soup From Scratch?
Can Honey Be A Salve for the Throat Chakra?
Bacon Isn't That Great, Why Do We So Fevrverently Insist It Is?

Is that even flirtation anymore?

Death's sweet winks.

Before all of it fell down like jenga slips. the drinking, again.

One day at a time or somebullshit like that.

Another Favor

you were so drunk during an aa zoom meeting in Australia that you closed eyed searched for one afternoon. You were called upon. No words but 'Here'

Where I belong

The cook dropped you off at your dad's once, murmurs of his wife and newborn on the way. He told you that *the secret to our gravy is that we add bacon grease to it*. **i'll never eat there.**

Your hands were shaking by 9pm. Withdrawals. Clock work.

On another favordrive home, he mentions Walden, you tell him you used to write poetry.

You thanked him for the ride home. He said anytime.

You went to your small room in your dads molding house, and cried on your twin bed on the concrete carpet floor

As your father sat silent, unknowing, in the room over.

just tiny vodka bottles at your feet to soothe the rip of vocal cord that is the word *used*.

Knife Parties

I've been fascinated with self affliction for as long as I can remember. The carnal being of humanity.

Love is Christmas,

The way my sister sings songs from 'O, Brother Where Art Thou' to her youngest daughter, in the armchair of our shared childhood home

Bathtub in the next room calling out memories of trauma is christmas.

I was lost on All-Port Street when she called, I wish my phone had died instead. It just rang and rang.

Haunted—Months too late.

I wanted my very own Christmas, just for me.

I still do

I miss train rides trading Wild Irish Roses, too drunk to get off at the right stop, having to take the L a lap again.

The girl with the boyfriend that you wanted to absorb because his words were like Christmas.

Can you take your newly bought pawn store knife and help me cut this wrapping paper?

There's better uses for it than it to be at my neck.

Ellie

The invention of the heart is also the invention of heartbreak. *How did it get so cold so fast?* The invention of knives is also the invention of knife wounds. *Why am I still not getting the right sizes in dressings?* The invention of love is the invention of me, on your mind at *three* o' clock on the dot. Why not *two*?
The invention of a lie is the invention of the 'truth'. Why is it never real for *you*?

Do you go out and paint the stars at night or did I dream that?

She is a liar and mean but I don't think anything is bad about that because that is my mother and my AP psychology teacher said that mothers were excruciatingly crucial in children's lives.
I am the problem? Is she the problem?

Isn't that Stockholm syndrome? Shredded girl asks the therapist this, pretending to have been sober for two weeks when she'll inevitably go to the bar down the stairs and across the small street.

Am I sick? Or is she? Or can we be both, separately? Is this why?
Can I go back into the womb and ask to undo the umbilical cord?
I'll make a new one. I will.
I wrote so long ago that I am a separate gene. I stand by that until my ankles falter and I, become yellow bellied; a cherry spitter Canary.

Sacrimony

According to urban dictionary— it is ceremony and sacrifice

The two unlikely dovetails

caught kissing, cheek to cheek, flushed red. caught.

Aching like the cabernet stashed in Our Father's Holy Ghost cabinet.

Triangulation.

There's a three point system to most everything you do:

Feeling. Thought. And Reaction.

Happenstance. — to shoot the second arrow is

Mental armament. Suffering in the end.

Release. Rise. Fall. Rise again.

Combat sports focus on using this to release something into the ether— interia.

An object at stays at rest. Sometimes it comes as

Exuberance.

Red petals being cast upon the ground is another way of surrender it seems.

Wave your white flag, I'll throw the petals down so you can delicately walk back.

Isn't that what it's about —

Oneness?

Did you count the steps as you walked up the stucco to find me?

Surrounded by dozens of echoes?

The way is through, but it's always easier than it seems.

THE COUNTRY OF YOU

and your sister, 7 p.m. in the kitchen of your childhood home as: requested, making a small portion of reheated spaghetti dinner.

Your mother down the vinyl wood paneled hallway, as she recovers from surgery.

The addict of you, stoned, fighting the shakes again or too much nicotine. Some things you don't tell yourself.

- Your sister, irritable, stirs the noodles, puts it back in the microwave. Radiating the meat and noodles. Tomatoes. *You're just standing there You're too stoned, Beth.*
- *I* don't wanna be here,
- I'm suffocating when I'm sober.
- Do I have to spell out to you the suffering or do you know too?

I'm fine.

Get me the salt and pepper

For **what?**

You stop moving your hand, errorless for once, reaching to the top of the overcrowded cupboards above the stove. Suspended. Haha, suspended. latin, sub, pendere. 4 years paid off in a weird way. No Law school but you sure as hell can fucking remember your roots. Focus, focus.

Her spaghetti.

Gross.

She's always done that.

Always needed. Always took.

Yes, you're right, yes, I remember now, she always has.

THE WOUNDED CHILD OF YOU

At the exact same time your sister is moving the noodles in the orange Tupperware bowl— you are not wanting to believe what the therapists are saying: Narcissistic Personality Disorder. It rolls off the tongue like a designer feature in a car.

This model has so much narcissism in it, it'll take you around the town and back and you will feel like you've traveled the world.

In the kitchen again, remembering how you always hated eating,

it's a burden too much anyway, can I just exist, cleanly? without fueling the car? What if I wanna see
how long it rolls?

If this goes in the mouth, and alters its posion.

You always eat as if someone's going to take your fucking food. You hated spaghetti, though.

Bright orange stains in tupperware makes for a good reason to have a meltdown. The smell. The steam of the huge pot in the small kitchen. (Why is it the men that remind you of your father the most, the ones with quiet anger.) The trashcan of tupperware aftermath.

Dog whistles.

In the strip club you worked in on and off for years, the chef had spaghetti every thursday. he would smoke his Marlboro reds, drink 44 ounces of Coke three times every night, somehow; Whiskey was his drink of choice after work at the bar you two would always go to. Up. Neat.

The Bartender there raped you one of your last worst drunks
He unpacks the cigarettes you buy, before, with this knowing stare.
Birds of a feather.

That's what kitchens in strip clubs are for—crying—along with, dressing rooms, the champagne rooms when the men go to the ATMS, bar scouting the bartender who watches the stage too intently at times, or bathrooms confettied with mystery magic powder on the backs of the toilets, quickly and quietly or to drink more.— to gulp it down.
Your choice. Usually both.

Richard, the cook, was the only man you let see you actually cry over men, how mean, kind, beautiful, terrible and small they could be for years.

Do you twirl or poke? **I twirl. Of course, I always twirl. Who else for? What else am I to do but twirl, for you, for her, for them, myself.**
It's all fun and games until I get dizzy again.

My therapist told me I need to work on communication. How does someone open their mouth if all they've even been inclined to do is shut it? I sing the songs over and over, they are just probably off key.
Dog whistles. They always come. In packs.

SHANNON

'i think my mother may be a trigger in my drinking.'
'i think that's a good observation, why do you think that'

Remember when I sat crying on the hallway floor, you're omnipresent you should,

When you left me at 18, momma bird leaving baby too soon

3 doors down from a man who stole the child in me away eleven years old on a too bright Sunday? Mark was there, Must've been sunday

You left again the day after I told you what he did, the war footage found, you love me?

Do people leave the ones they love this much? Is it always like this? Is that normal?

Do people just go? Did I do that? Will I do that? How do I stop?

I stopped Drinking & Killing myself

Do you recall when I told you I was a month sober and you still made it about you.

Sometimes I tell you I love you just to reassure myself, it's all one sided in a way. True masochism.

Pain is the best teacher.

I wish I had known you would die.

I wish I had known you would die.

I wish I had known you would have died before I did.

Graveyard

The first love I ever had that loved me back and I believed him who I
would push away like clock work said it best: you crave to be hurt.
You're good at it. My best talent.
Not in a cruel way, it was pillow talk. An acceptance of my fate.

His fingers in my mouth and my mind worried about car oil on his
fingers.
Claws of my mind.

I remember hands best out of anyone. Especially his.
If someone touches me once and then later, again, I remember. My
body is trained to memorize them.

The hell I bring with me is undeserved.
Me coming home from work at the local casino at 10 A.M.
Graveyard angel

His break at work at 10:30, waiting on classes at noon, editing 10
page essays I wrote half-asleep the evening before, quick sex in our
small apartment bathroom while he was supposed to be having
lunch.
It was usually me instead.

My grandma keeps asking me who I'd marry out of all the men I've
seen. I sigh.
It was him. His name would fall out my mouth. Until recently.
Now I choose me. Not him.

The prize rabbit at the fair. pretty and not to be touched.
Never again. Nestling on her trophy, atop a mirror.
Kinder than she's ever experienced.

Chicago Fever Dream

The electrician that would come in every second Tuesday of the
month, clockwork
His hands were rough, but damn, did he have great hands and a
better etiquette told you'd take you away and for a second you
believed it.

*Why are hands grabbing your hips so erotic when you have control? Is
it about control? Or the idea of it? Can you save you from you? How
do you save someone from themselves?*

There were so many men

Jake from Louisiana. One leg, beaten down. Actor eyes. He took
you to New Orleans; Slowly killing you and himself. You were 22.
He was 36. Too young to know better, they told me. Only your best
friend knew where you were.

The man with the son with Cerebral Palsy, who you called daddy
on occasion during lap dances, because he asked you to and tipped
so well. It made your skin crawl but it was also writing home to a
father you couldn't speak to.

Traitorous woman.

Louis, sad man, broken life, two dollar stage tipper. everytime.

Your big night. the most money you've made in an hour.
The aquarium in the room was your favorite thing about the
experience. You cried in the bathroom when the men were signing
receipts at the bar to go to the room. the girl going with you to the
room went with you, kept telling you deserved it. you kept telling
her no you didn't, no, it's not supposed to be *me*, trying to not mess
up your makeup while wiping away tears with shaking hands.

The man from Denver-- in town on some fucking business trip.
Lunch break quickies. You remember those.
He paid you $100 to sit on his lap and let him just hold you after
long talks over screwdrivers and Merlot about: New York, Sex
Work, Power, Women, Men, Money, Fetish Work, Being A Man,
Being a Stripper, The South, Chicago Transplation, Uprooting, His
Kids, Wife, Home is, What Home Can't Be, Shame, Guilt,
Remorse, and Desire.

6 minutes is a long time to be held by a man you just met,

Kissing his cheek at the end, thanking him as he left at the end of
the hour for the answers he hadn't told you yet.

Vivisection

Fingers spiders on the fretboard
Remember how you broke up
with a pair of hands and 32 teeth
Because tarot possessed you to
Burn the image of skylines into your skin
like a psoriasis flare

Remember how she lied about safety being something she'd
provide?
Blood oath taken back at momentary notice.

What if I played a game, but I did not agree to tell you the rules
What parts of you would still say yes?
Name them, braid their hair.
They deserve it.

7 year old uses bathroom door knob trick in local
buffett— pizza buffet — lost piece of body—string mommy
brought— she chose chocolate dessert pizza after

My oldest part of me says, good girls belong on their knees.

I, however, reside perched on a man's spine.
Contrast ache. I remember too much.
Rope burns baby better, remember?
The heel of my shoe skidding in places
His wife will see later.

A testament to a love story made up in my head

It's always on the tip of the tongue-- little wiggly baby tooth, the spot in the room where the light catches its own wave lengths.
Watching you through the curio cabinet is ballet. The progression of a fever. What a show the fine china we will never use, gets to see.
Thrown blankets over chairs get to feel the way your fingers frisk with futile intention. I love just watching people, how they move when they think no one's watching-- it's a weird intimacy. I fawn over it.

The picture on the wall remembering how shaky your hands were putting them up. You were always so detail orientated. Safe in your grip, as always.

Stoned on your couch, lessons in stitching, and gravity. I was so intentional. Grappling with Slyvia not to devour you on my plate and Nabokov's Vera to lick the backs of your stamps.

Remember when I told you I was scared

This is what I was talking about.

Crown Shyness

"Phenomenon observed in some trees where the crowns of fully stocked trees do not touch each other, forming a canopy with channel like gaps."

You, carpenter hands, Jesus calling you to commend to knees and take hammer to nail.
Teeth to woodskin.
cicadas hum when you release. can't you hear it?
the small bruise on my neck of a craving too strong, too heavyweight, like your high gravity beers.
I want your passionflowers, only.
can your godhands plant me in my soil where I belong rightfully?

sacred, my rituals, my compulsions, the smell of wine, my body. something Jesus could condemn me on.
My follow through is impressive.
Here I am again, undressing in the mirror for myself, and you somewhere in the still of night— male
fantasies, male fantasies, male fantasies— Margaret would wag her finger

The space between want and need is crownshyness.
I danced to songs in the late night, under venus spinning in rampant urgency, about halos slipping down.
my halo is between want and need.
i won't have to spell that out for you.
The gap between my thighs is the perfect size for your carpenter hands. Ring fittings in small bathrooms.

ribbons as restraints, save the leather for a later date; I tied myself in the best bow, just for you—
hungry— to rip open, christmas was like fire they will be thereafter, as long as you fall from fingers, as they dripdry.

the god of my choosing is uninvited to this part —your confessional box is out of order.
Tell me your sins and I'll show you how to pray about them a bit better.

VENUS IN DIALOGUE

your mother must be so proud, published and everything, what's a pretty
smart girl doing in a place like this?
They tell me. minutes after me spewing a dress rehearsal: I write, I think I
would disappear if I stopped. I don't share my poetry with strange men in
the dark. youngest of three. no kids. No, I think god invented me to be
alone. Thank you. I think the sky is meant for me.

How long have you been doing this, he asks

Breathing or being enticing? Giving you the control? Knowing or
unconsciously?
Are you a force of nature, or am I?
Did you know I have a freckle in my right eyeball? No, it's not detrimental.
It's just there.
Here, let me read your palms: we can talk about how long you've been here,
doing this instead.
Reading futures under neon lights holds a different kind of intimacy.
Can I prove to you - to myself- that I claim myself and can still have you in
my periphery
The correct question you should be asking is: how long have I felt this way?

Can I fuck you?
No.
Can you fuck me?
No.
Are you wet right now?
no.
Do you like this?
If I say yes, you will not stop. If I say no, you will not stop. It's chess. I
move, you move. You have to try not to remove your queen, she is a fixture
in your life. Mother dearest. Your nights are moving solely in a
L-shape.
Don't risk the queen-- it's 10 points.
Am I losing?
Yes
How can you tell?

it's perpetual. inevitable.

How long have you been doing this?

I bruise knees over and over-- to prove to myself, once again that I am perpetually fading, like the bruises.

I've always asked for marks, but never quite get the one I want.

ON JAKE—

You fucked a man who had a 15 year old son.

consensually—you were drunk but still was attracted to him. His voice, velvety deer antlers, the story he had: lost a leg, a business, wife, but still fucking kickin'

his potential. Remember that? Potential.

He never let you call him daddy, it was strange for the both of you. Back to father you will always go.

You know what they say: Prey is always on its

knees

Recall shot for shot, a young colt coated in Louisiana guilt, selective homophobia, lengthy angry men, highballs and whiskey sours. Hard man with a gooey center.

Sugar on the tongue melting in summer swelter.

False father he became. as always, as they do.

eyes blue like your niece's hands, when she transferred from womb to world. Inconsolable.

You kept picking at your skin, one night, drunken mumbling with Jack Daniels, a sweet kiss on the lips, sitting in his enclosed garage, rain tapping the metal.

You ask him if love is real.

He said probably not.

In one of the fever dreams he gave you, you saw a younger version of yourself: wild child, unbridled, knives twirling, cotton mouthed.

Wind winding around you like cling wrap.

In the dunes, one of the hardest things to keep out of your mouth is fruit flies.

When you are an alcoholic, your sweat becomes sweet—

His tiled kitchen had so many ants in the summer

You tell him that he is wrong about love. He knows this. You know he knows this. It fits into the pockets of your teeth, you say, into the pores of your forehead, gives you sugar headaches.

Doesn't your jaw lock?

Lin Elizabeth is a 27 year old sober poet, born in the soft underbelly belly of the Arkansasan River Valley. Her works touch on the inner wounding of addiction, mother trauma, and the stark light that is sobriety. Her poems have appeared in *Basset Hound Press, Titled House Magazine, Goat's Milk Magazine, The Idle Class, Applause Magazine, Hypertrophic Press, Dream Boy Book Club,* and *Secondchance Review.*

Found on instagram at @borrowedpotpourri

ACKNOWLEDGEMENTS

I would like to thank my readers, I am endlessly grateful for you My grandmother, my father, my sister, my brother, my sponsors, my beautiful community in both AA and NA, Hailee C for the tattoo scandal. That was the most fun I've ever had sober. The oleander will be carried with me until I die. Michael S, thank you for being my kindred spirit in the scary rooms, thank you for letting me mouth the words of the lord's prayer and keeping that sacred. Jake, always. Don H, Ron M, Sherry D, Cindy G, Alex Z my first and most special. The list goes on ad infinitum until we run out of alcoholics. My sangha, you bless me more than I will be able to adequately express. My friends, those who pushed me to write this, the man that prayed in the restaurant alone, my mother and the lessons she kept, Dawn Carpenter, you've saved me more with your graciousness than any human ever has. I sincerely owe my life to you. Eva Woods for diagnosing my mother, and tenderly letting me fall apart. Chip Lovvorn, rest in love, Kody Ford, you are the best person I have ever met; Christian, for letting me skip prompts in poetry workshop and reminding her that men are men and will do things that men do for a timid forever, and nieces and nephew for keeping me safe and sometimes sane and always sober. I thank Margaret Atwood for her knowledge, and the generosity of it.

I would also like to thank, finally, the alcoholic that this speaks to — you are not alone. You keep me sober. You have harborship in me.

The amount of gratitude I have for those of you who are afflicted by life and it's sometimes damned circumstance is beyond human capacity to explain.